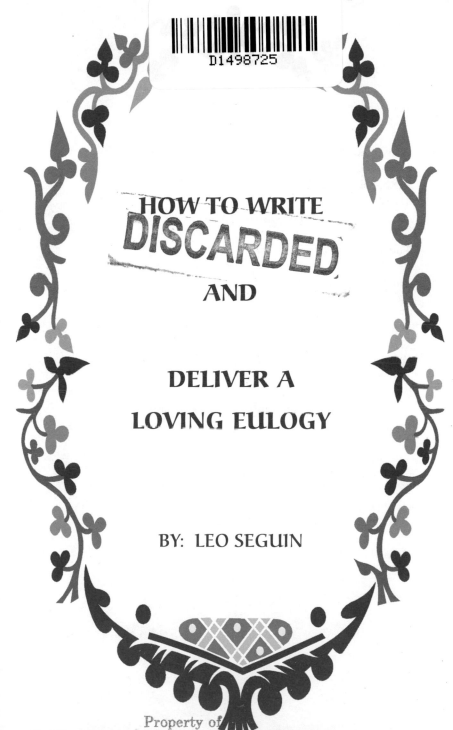

FEB 21 2006

D1498725

HOW TO WRITE
DISCARDED,
AND

DELIVER A
LOVING EULOGY

BY: LEO SEGUIN

Copyright 1997
Second Revised edition 1999
L.P.S. Publishing
10712-101 Street
Westlock, Ab Canada
T7P 1H7
Phone #   (780) 349-3300
Fax #   (780) 349-6301
Toll Free   1-877-460-0053
email   eulogy@telusplanet.net

Leo Seguin (1950)
How to Write and Deliver a Loving Eulogy
ISBN 0-9684169-0-X

1. Eulogy   2. Self-Help   3. Reference

Printed in Canada
Friesens Printing

Contents

ACKNOWLEDGMENTS

To My Family
Bonnie, Jeffrey, Jason, Heidi and Matthew

To My Parents
Flora and Wilfrid

To The Good Lord for Giving Them To Me

To My Good Friend
Glen Semenchuk
For Moulding and Polishing This Book

To
Jo-Anne Borduzak
For Deciphering and Typing This Work

GOAL - MISSION

When asked by family or friends to deliver a eulogy, there is usually very little time for planning. This book is designed as a guide to help you build and deliver a loving eulogy.

It will provide, in a concise form, a vehicle of expression produced with empathy and compassion. The prose will be constructed from your own personal thoughts, your generous emotions, your caring hands, hands imbued with loyalty and worthy purpose (using our tools) you are a child of God. There never was anyone quite like you, there never will be for time to come. This uniqueness is you, it's beautiful, don't forsake it for anything.

This guide will allow you to more easily accomplish the task at hand. It comes with an outline of information gathering, the process of organization, the step by step manual of assembly and the theme of neighbourly concern and love!

When you are done you will feel like you have delivered from your mind and heart a love capsule to the minds and hearts of family and friends with you as a spokesperson - a final gift of praise to the dearly departed!

INTRODUCTION

The dictionary describes a eulogy as a speech of high praise about someone, often times a person who unfortunately has passed on.

I don't believe there are many greater honours in this world that could be bestowed on someone than putting together an actual summation and reflection of a person's life.

An honour, reserved for the closest, most trustworthy, most respected of friends, an undertaking few pursue, but one which when accepted can yield some of the greatest feelings of pride and satisfaction you will ever experience. You are held in the highest of esteem by these people because you have been entrusted with the job of reflecting on this person's life, a life possession they more than likely cherished more than any thing else on earth. It is one of the most unselfish projects you will ever undertake because quite frankly, for these few days, you will be placing the concern of others before your very own.

You should be commended for accepting this task, but like many new experiences, it can bring on a bit of anxiety. This anxiety is good and when properly captured can be one of your greatest allies. In the ensuing chapters, I will show you how to harness this productive power especially if you are travelling alone. The best way to alleviate that problem is travel with a friend. Let this book be your travelling companion and partner, helping you reach a successful conclusion, always confronting every indecision head on.

CHAPTER 1

GATHERING INFORMATION

CHAPTER 1

GATHERING-INFORMATION

Our aim in this chapter, simple yet so important, is to gather as much information about this individual as possible and to select the appropriate items. This must be accomplished within the confines of a restrictive time frame as most funeral services are held within four days after the passing of the dearly departed.

During the course of this person's life they have displayed various foibles and weaknesses, but this is not what is to be selected. Speak all the good you can of people. The ingredients of a eulogy have to be fresh, they have to be of correct quantity and carefully selected. They should include:

1. Positive knowledge of this individual, as much as we can acquire...Where?? From the experts on this subject...family, friends, co-workers, acquaintances and, others. Schedule a meeting with the family and others as soon as possible, start this process now.

2. Delve into your own experiences. Ask your subconscious to start bringing forth your own recollection of this person. This process is slow, always carry a pen and a note pad allowing you to record this information as it occurs to you.

3. If possible attempt to acquire other eulogies (find Actual Eulogies-Chapter VIII) and advice from people who have also faced this same challenge.

This standard format of organizing your information may act as a guide:

      1. Opening

2. History (Birth, Parents-dates, etc.)
3. Family
4. Friends
5. Volunteerism-Community Involvement
6. Profession-Career
7. Hobbies
8. Praise
9. End
10. General

To obtain information from other people, I have included questionnaires which will work as guides. These questionnaires flow into your previous categories, so as this information comes in, keep it in separate file folders.

When speaking to or interviewing people, keep it as informal as possible. Record as quickly as you can to capture as much as you can. I will show you how to do the final organization of this material in Chapter V.

GENERAL QUESTIONNAIRE

Things you need to know so you can continue to grow!

BACKGROUND

Time and Date of Service: _____

Location of Facility:_____

Address: _____

Do you need a map: Yes_____ No_____

Person in charge of facility: _____

Phone Number and Name: _____

Best times to contact: _____

Questions of Facility Manager:

Would it be okay to come and practise:Yes_____ No_____

Do you have a public address system: Yes _____ No _____

Do you have a podium: Yes _____ No _____

Name of clergy if not the same: _____

Phone number: _____

Best time to contact: _____

QUESTIONS

What length of eulogy is appropriate?

_____

At what point in the service would you like me to present it?

_____

Can you give me some sort of signal?

_____

Do you have a specific place you want me to sit?

_____

FAMILY

Did you want me to make announcements at the end of the eulogy regarding:

Coffee or lunch to follow? Yes _____ No _____

Private burial or other? Yes _____ No _____

Thank people on behalf of family for coming?

 Yes_____ No _____

Come to house, etc.? Yes _____ No _____

Other: _____

_____

(If they so desire you can become spokesperson for Family at lunch, etc)

Family contact: _____

Phone Number: _____

Address: _____

Family member who is going to do history: _____

_____

Phone Number: _____

Time and place I will get the history: _____

_____

(Remember to use Questionnaire. This will prove to be very help-ful to them.)

Do they want extra copies of eulogy for family: If yes ____, how many copies?_____

Do they want copies of eulogy for service: If yes ____, how many copies? _____

If there are two services, do they want a eulogy at both serv-ices? Yes____No____

Is there something special, a poem or song they would like to include? Yes _____ No_____

Is there something from family and friends, they would like to include? Yes _____ No _____

"Is their anything I haven't mentioned that I might be able to help you with?" Always remembering family is bereaved and they will appreciate this gesture. This detailed approach insures everyone is comfortable and nothing is forgotten.

_____

_____

_____

_____

_____

_____

_____

_____

_____

QUESTIONNAIRES

HISTORY

If a person is a long time resident it may not be necessary to detail every aspect of his or her lineage. This is a suggested history guideline, you and the family should always discern how much information is to be included. A knowledgeable family member, can help ensure that it is accurate. Review with them the pronunciation of all names. Fill in the blanks and disregard information that doesn't apply.

FAMILY

_____,
name

one of _____ children, was born _____
date

to _____
parents

of _____
address/town

He/She is survived by:

SISTERS:

Names	*Addresses*

BROTHERS:

Names	*Addresses*

_____

_____

_____

_____

_____

He/she was predeceased by parents yes/no _____ sisters/
brothers, yes/no, if yes include names here:

_____

_____

EDUCATION:

_____ attended _____
          Name   *Type*

School in_____
                              Location

and later completed _____SCHOOL
                                 Name

in _____ Post Secondary at
                 Type

_____

CAREER

In _____, _____
           Date   *Name*

  began his/her career working, started business, etc.

for _____

later, he/she worked at _____

MARRIAGE

In_____, _____met _____
   Date   *Name*   *Spouse*

Courtship details, if any, how did they meet _____

_____

_____

_____

Date married _____

CHILDREN

    Name of Child   *Date of Birth*   *Spouses Name*

_____

_____

_____

_____

_____

_____

GRANDCHILDREN   (if there are a large number you may want to mention in mass) with other relatives and friends, or

NAMES   DAUGHTER(S)/SON(S) OF

_____

_____

_____

_____

_____

_____

_____

_____

_____

_____

End: Please file under history for later retrieval.

QUESTIONNAIRE - FAMILY

As you are going through these questionnaires we encourage you to take a quick look at descriptive words pages 28 to 32 and circle those which apply to this individual. This will be of help when you get to the Chapter VIII-Organizing.

When you are meeting with family, try to get as many family members together as you can in a short period of time. At this meeting, in an informal way begin the discussion by utilizing the Family Questionnaire. Be ready because the information will come quickly and profusely.

FAMILY MEETING QUESTIONNAIRE

ie: - are just examples use your own appropriate words

Was _____ a

_____

ie: honourable, loyal, generous, devoted, loving spouse

_____

_____

_____

_____

_____

_____

Did they have a strong marriage built on mutual respect, etc.? _____

_____

_____

_____

_____

Was he/she the glue and spirit of the home? Devoted to

each other through good times and bad?

_____

_____

_____

_____

_____

How would you best describe them as husband and wife?
Were they life partners, ie: thoughtful, kind, romantic? Other
questions and answers.

_____

_____

_____

Was _____ a

_____

  ie: principled, strong, dedicated, caring, compassionate
parent, a good example, did he/she establish and instill high
ethics and morals in an appropriate value system. Did he/
she leave the great gift of a good name to his/her children?
Did he/she place concern of children-parents before their
own? How would you sum up in a word, phrase, paragraph
the essence of this person? Was family No. 1 to this individual? Was he/she humble, humorous?

_____

_____

_____

_____

_____

_____

_____

Was he/she devoted, close to grandchildren?

_____

_____

_____

_____

Was he/she a

_____

ie: creative, organized, inspiring, mentor

as a brother, sister, uncle, aunt

_____

_____

_____

Was time with family the happiest time for this individual?

_____

_____

_____

Please remember to include stories anecdotes, humorous incidents that would help to portray these character traits. Harmony at home translates itself into effectiveness everywhere and in many cases is the core, the centre of many individuals lives.

FRIENDS QUESTIONNAIRE

Friendship is one of the greatest assets a person can ever have or hope to have! It is a flow of love in both directions, giving while receiving, receiving while giving! Explain to these individuals you have been given the honour of presenting the eulogy and would they mind assisting.

What kind of friend was _____ to you was he/she

_____
ie: true, forgiving, humble, warm, loving, joyful, close

_____

_____

_____

_____

_____

Was he/she there since your youth? Through thick and thin? Always there for you? Helped you when you were down or sick?

_____

_____

_____

_____

_____

In a word, phrase, paragraph, how would you describe this individual? What did they mean to you?

_____

_____

_____

_____

Is there a short message you would like to include?

_____

_____

_____

Is there a story, anecdote, humorous incident you might suggest may be of interest?

_____

_____

_____

_____

_____

_____

VOLUNTEERISM-COMMUNITY INVOLVEMENT
QUESTIONNAIRE

To be used to interview his/her cohorts, officers or executive members that worked with he/she in these fields of endeavour. Was he/she a reliable, dedicated, unfaltering, loyal member of the

_____

ie. organization

for _____ years of service. Through the course of these

_____ years he/she served as _____

_____

ie: president for two terms and as secretary for one term

He/she also received

_____

ie: award

_____

_____

What type of member was he/she: always there to lend a hand, very humble, always enthusiastic, the reason he/she achieved a sincere concern for the community?

_____

_____

_____

_____

_____

In a word, sentence, anecdote, how would you best describe this individual?

_____

_____

_____

Some of the greatest joys on earth come when serving others!

PROFESSION QUESTIONNAIRE

Use to interview fellow workers, clients, business acquaintances, etc.

He/she

_____

ie: hardworking, ambitious, determined, capable, persevering, etc.

_____

_____

_____

Was he/she

_____

ie; respected, admired, appreciated

by the people they shared employment with or their clients, students, colleagues, etc.

_____

_____

_____

Did he/she have an unusual talent or respected craft that was

_____

ie: superior, outstanding, etc. or showed strength, or integrity

_____

_____

Were they _____ by their peers?
       ie: loved, admired or appreciated

_____

_____

_____

Is their an incident of these characteristics that would help us to paint a word picture of this person? Was he/she a diligent worker, respectful of the feelings of others, great team player?

_____

_____

_____

_____

_____

Was he/she a good provider?

_____

_____

_____

How would you best describe his/her most positive attributes?

_____

_____

_____

_____

_____

*A person who on a daily basis finds work that he/
she truly enjoys is indeed a happy person.*

HOBBIES-PASTIME   QUESTIONNAIRE

What did this individual enjoy doing with their spare time?

_____

ie: travelling, golfing, fishing, hockey, reading, playing the piano, etc.

_____

_____

_____

_____

Did he/she have unusual talents as it relates to these activities?

_____

_____

_____

Was he/she happiest when they were doing these things with family and friends?

_____

_____

Other comments regarding pastimes.

_____

_____

_____

Free time is a gift from God.

PRAISE QUESTIONNAIRE

Use with anyone who you feel can help to form a picture of this person's best qualities. This questionnaire, I hope, will be the precious key that will unlock the door to this individual's inner storehouse and enable you to reflect and gain his/her true essence, true self worth. Here we praise his/hers finest qualities, best talents, most worthwhile attributes. Build them up! Happy are those who build others up!

He/she was a very warm, special, generous, devoted person, he/she never judged anyone, placed well being of others before their own self. Main goal - take time to brighten others lives, loved to praise, to laugh. Great friend, courageous, brave, kind. Was the best dad, best mom in the world, was compassionate and humble, had tremendous talent for painting, cooking, etc, true goodness, steadfast.

_____

_____

_____

_____

_____

_____

_____

_____

Is their an attribute that you would say would permeate every aspect of this person's life?

_____

_____

_____

_____

Can you give us a word, a paragraph an anecdote or story that would help to capture these special qualities?

_____

_____

_____

_____

_____

_____

_____

In many cases the most beautiful aspects of people are hidden within, work hard to capture this most beautiful aspect of human life!

CHAPTER 11

Yes
No

CHAPTER 11

YES - NO

F ind included here some observations made over the course of many years that I hope will help you along this journey.

YES

1. Skim through this book as soon as you can. Take note it is written in the exact order events should be undertaken to ensure your success. These are the same logical thought patterns an individual uses in communicating an idea to someone.

2. Be Positive - use praise, after all, you are speaking about one of God's children.

3. Check carefully about any specifics, special rules, or regulations about facility or religious beliefs involved.

4. Yes, humour can be used but exercise extreme caution here, use only if it relates to this specific person. If there is any chance it will offend, don't use it! I used humour on Page 64 (V. Curtis) relating to her always being late. This is how I stated it "Punctuality, as many of you know, was not one of Virginia's strong suits." (People laughed) Humour often fits if the person had a good sense of humour and as such is a distinct part of that individual. Never use humour at someone else's expense, if used it should always be kind.

5. Yes, be extremely compassionate, the bereaved are under extreme stress, be understanding, be caring. Do everything in your power to lighten their load, making this burden easier to carry.

6. Gather the information you require as quickly as possible. There is nothing better than being well prepared. It's a great confidence builder.

7. Try to delegate or relinquish any responsibilities you may have in the time leading up to the service.

8. Yes, check early on in the process with the Cleric or Pastor as to length of your talk, or any other advice or direction he may have to give you.

9. Yes, find a quiet place to prepare this eulogy. No phone, no distractions - this is especially true when you get to Chapter V - Organization. You need some quiet, undisturbed time where you can really focus in on the job at hand. It may have to be when everyone is gone to bed, but I can assure you of one thing, the quieter it is the quicker you will be done.

NO

1. Say no to using highly technical language that people won't understand.

2. Never bring up any type of material or past situation that might be even remotely construed as controversial. Your best judge here is common sense and the best rule of thumb is never use anything that may hurt anyone's feelings.

3. When singling out or mentioning close friends or family, use careful evaluation because someone left out may feel they were much closer than those talked about. Sometimes it might be better not to specifically mention anyone but rather to generalize.

4. Say no in most circumstances to leaving a family member out because of a past wrong. Let the congregation and God be the judge, after all they did exist.

5. Say no to temptation of making a presentation too long (10-12 minutes normal length). By being well organ-

ized, concise and to the point, you will satisfy two basic needs; first, the need of the clergy to **maintain the constraints of their normal service length and second you will be admired for presenting a word portrait of the deceased in a concise accurate form.**

6. Say no to over embellishing this individuals accomplishments, (don't indicate they were a pillar of the community when actually they were much less than that). Every person has some good within them. Focus on these areas and use unlimited praise but be realistic. Let's face it people are smart, they would see through that in a second!

7. Don't worry about accumulating too much material. In Chapter V - Organization, we will work on the premise that it is easier to discard than revisit for more information.

CHAPTER III

Making It Special

CHAPTER III

MAKING IT SPECIAL

As you can well imagine over the years millions of eulogies have been given, most have been of an average nature, some have been extraordinary. I want yours to be of the latter variety.

For an extraordinary work to occur, the gathering must be made to feel that a message of impassioned vitality is being transferred from the heart, mind and soul of the eulogist to the heart, mind and soul of the congregation. It occurs with the inner fire of burning desire, using the hot coals of unrelenting zeal, the fuel of self discipline and hard work, fanned by the motivating breeze of service to family and friends above self.

No doubt you know the bereaved well, you are close to the family. Remember this is a difficult time for them, you want to help them through this. Let that love, that concern, that emotion show through. Let it be an indicator of the caring that will yield a powerful, inspiring, joyful result.

Following are some ideas that will help to make your eulogy special:

1. The easiest way to start that fire is by using one the greatest ingredients on earth, enthusiasm, as only you yourself can do it. There is always a tendency in public speaking to try and imitate or copy someone else. Resist that temptation for it steals from you, your individuality, your uniqueness. This uniqueness is you, it's beautiful, be proud of it. It is the spark that will light the real life impassioned fervour we call enthusiasm.

2. Another way to make your work exceptional is by adding your personal ingredients. I observed an example of this in a eulogy delivered about a highly respected and admired Grandmother. The eulogist had taken the time to speak to many of her Grandchildren, asking them to write in a sentence or two, their loving impression of this woman. He quoted them as saying "Grandma always took the time no matter how busy she was to listen, when we really needed her. Grandma was always giving of herself for the benefit of others."

    This same approach can be used as it relates to quotes from family and friends or utilize a poem or song that this person was particularly fond of. So put your own signature on this hand-crafted treasure, it will be one that the family will always cherish.

3. I encourage you to use real life, personal stories, to enhance and give a clear perspective of this individual's finest character traits. Examples may be "He was a kind, loving man who had great respect for God's animals." Story told about him finding a cat with a broken leg and how he took great care to nurse it back to health. "She was the most unselfish person I've ever met." Story told of how for six months she went through excruciating pain to provide skin grafts for her niece who had been severely burnt in a house fire.

4. Another very effective tool for adding eloquence is to find a golden thread, a common denominator that shines forth as one of that person's finest character traits. The greatest character trait in one lady I eulogized was her outstanding artistic ability, V. Curtis. I make reference to her being a beautiful canvas painted by the Master Artist himself, painted in the brightest of colours to reflect her cheerful, sunny disposition. Throughout this eulogy I utilized this common denominator to add spark, force and sincerity to the overall effect.

This process can serve as the camera, allowing the collective eye of the gathering to see first hand for themselves, the finest essence of this person's very being.

So this point in our journey we have established our goal, diligently collected loads of information and we have lit the fire of passion. We are well on our way to success!

CHAPTER IV

DESCRIPTIVE WORDS

CHAPTER IV

DESCRIPTIVE WORDS

ability
acclaimed
achieve
adequate
adversity
agile
all-around
ambition
analytical
appreciative
architect
artistic
astonishing
attentive
awake
beautiful
best
boisterous
breathtaking
brotherly
calm
careful
celebrity
character
charming
clean
close-knit
commendable
compassionate
complimentary
confidence
consistent
contented

able-bodied
accommodating
active
admirable
affable
agreeable
all-star
ambitious
ancestry
approachable
arresting
asset
astute
attractive
awesome
becoming
big-hearted
bold
bright
business-like
capable
caring
certain
charismatic
cheerful
clear-headed
cognisant
committed
compatible
concern
conscientious
constant
convincing

abundant
accomplishment
adapt
adventurous
affectionate
alert
amazing
amusing
angel
appropriate
articulate
assured
athletic
attribute
backbone
benevolent
blessed
brave
brilliant
busy
carefree
cautious
champion
charitable
classy
clear-sighted
coherent
common-thread
competent
concrete
considerate
constructive
cool-headed

co-operative	cordial	courageous
courteous	creative	credible
cultivated	daring	dashing
decent	decisive	dedicated
deft	deliberate	delicate
delighted	demure	dependable
desire	determined	devil-may-care
devoted	devotion	dignified diligent
direct	disarming	discreet
discipline	distinct	droll
duplicate	dynamic	eager
earnest	easy going	ebullient
ecstatic	educated	effective
efficient	effervescent	elated
elegant	eloquent	emotion
empathy	enchanted	energetic
engaging	enlightened	enterprising
enthusiastic	entrepreneur	established
esteem	esteemed	ethical
euphoric	even-handed	even-tempered
excellent	exceptional	expedite
experience	expert	exquisite
extraordinary	exuberant	fair
fair-minded	faith	famous
fantastic	far-sighted	fascinating
fashionable	fatherly	favorable
fearless	feisty	fervent
fierce	fiery	finefirm
first-string	flourish	focused
forgiving	formidable	forth-right
fortitude	fortunate	freefriendly
friendship	fun	fun-loving
generous	genial	gentlemen
gentlewoman	gifted	giving
glamorous	glorify	glowing
god-like	good-hearted	good-humoured
good-morals	good-natured	goodness
good-tempered	graceful	gracious
grateful	great	great-faith
great-hearted	gritty	gumption
gutsy	handsome	happy
hardy	hard-working	harmonious

heart-broken	heart-warming	heavenly
hero	heroine	heroism
high-minded	high-spirited	hilarious
holy	homemaker	honest
honesty	honorable	hope
hopeful	humanitarian	humble
humour	idealistic	imagination
immaculate	impassioned	impeccable
importance	important	incredible
individual	industrious	infectious
influential	informative	ingenuity
ingrained	initiative	innovative
inquisitive	inspiring	integrity
intellect	intellectual	intelligent
intuitive	invaluable	irrepressible
jovial	joyful	joyous
jubilant	just	kind
kind-hearted	kindness	laid-back
largest	laughing	leadership
learned	legendary	level
level-headed	likeable	light-hearted
lineage	lion-hearted	lively
logical	love	low-key
loyal	magnificent	major
manly	maternal	mature
marvellous	mighty	mild
moderate	modest	monumental
moral	motherly	motivated
natural	neighbourly	noble
no-nonsense	nurture	objective
obliging	open-hearten	open-minded
optimistic	orderly	organized
original	outgoing	outstanding
passionate	patience	patient
patriarch	peaceful	perceptive
perfectionist	perseverance	persevering
persistent	personable	personify petite
phenomenal	philanthropist	photogenic
playful	pleasant	polished
positive	potential	powerful
pragmatic	praise	pride
principled	principled-life	professionalism

proficient	profound	progressive
prominent	prompt	protective
proud	prudent	public-spirited
punctual	pure	purpose
qualified	quality	quick-witted
quiet	radiant	rational
reasonable	refined	reflective
relaxed	reliable	relentless
religious	reputable	reputation
resilient	resourceful	respected
resplendent	responsibility	responsible
responsive	revered	righteous
right-hand	rock-solid	robust
romantic	rugged	sacrificial
scholar	scrappy	self-confident
self-disciplined	self-effacing	self-forgetting
selfless	self-made	self-minded
self-reliant	self-sacrifice	self-sufficient
self-supporting	self-sustaining	sensible
sensitive	sentimental	serious-minded
sharing	sharp	significant
sincere	sisterly	skilful
smart	smooth	sociable
social-minded	soft-spoken	sophisticated
special	splendid	solid
spirited	sportsman-like	spotless
stately	staunch	statuesque
steadfast	steady	steward
strapping	strength	striking
strong	strong-minded	stunning
stupendous	sturdy	tactful
talented	tangible	temperate
tender	tenderness	thankful
thrifty	tireless	tough-minded
tremendous	triumphant	trust
trusting	trustworthy	truthful
unemotional	unencumbered	unfailing
unflappable	unflattering	unique
unruffled	untroubled	valiant
valuable	vibrant	vigilant
vigour	vigorous	vintage
vital	vitality	virtuous

visionary	vivacious	volatile
volunteer	warm	warm-hearten
welcome	well-done	well-groomed
well-informed	well-intentioned	well-mannered
well-meaning	well-rounded	wholehearted
wholesome	winner	winning
wonderful	work	workmanlike
worldly	worthy	worthwhile
youthful		

CHAPTER V

ORGANIZATION

CHAPTER V

ORGANIZATION

The ability to organize has often been recognized as one of the most important ingredients necessary for success. The world, unfortunately, is filled with many highly intelligent people who through the course of their life accomplish very little. The reason, in many cases, is their own personal human organization lacks a capable manager to combine, harmonize and put in order these productive ideas. The brain is a wondrous device offering to it's owner hundreds of magnificent ideas a day, but these ideas are like a boat without a compass, drifting aimlessly. They like so much air, will dissipate never to have the opportunity of achieving material status.

This is exactly where we find ourselves now in this equation, at a cross-roads, being fully cognizant of the fact we have taken a very important step. We haven't fretted any of those ideas away, have we. No, we have them locked away in the secure storehouse of our filing system.

When you get to this final construction stage you need some additional tools:

-scissors
-scotch tape
-stapler
-lined paper
-cue cards (required next chapter)
-master list (Page 2)
-felt pens - 2 or 3 different colours
-highlighters - 2 or 3 different colours
-file folders - 8 - 10 (split up categories)
-thesaurus (nice to have)
-dictionary
-list of descriptive words
(Chapter IV Page 28, saves you time)

-large table or desk
-well lit, quiet location
-lower than normal room temperature if possible
(you think better)

Okay, so we're ready, we have our tools now laid out on a large well lit desk, in a quiet room, surrounded by an abundance of information. Now you would never think of taking off on a strange trip without a map or building a house without a blueprint. I am pleased to provide this for you, look to Page 2 for your master shopping list. As we continue on this journey keep it close at hand. It is probably at this point that you will want to take a moment to review and modify this list to fit your subject's individuality and the desires of the family, coupled with the order you want to use delivering your eulogy.

Now another crucial bit of information, a rule of thumb, which will determine how aggressively you have to analyse your information. The eulogies I have included in this book are about ten to twelve minutes in duration, depending on your voice speed, or about 800-900 words total. Now you've talked to the clergyman in charge, they have indicated an approximate allotment of time for you in the service, say it is ten minutes.

Take a look at the master list, let's do a rough breakdown based on number of words for each category.

Word Count
1. Opening	50
2. History	50
3. Family	150
4. Friends	100
5. Volunteerism-Community Involvement	100
6. Profession-Career	100
7. Hobbies	125
8. Praise	125
9. End - Close	50
10. General	50
TOTAL	850

Your breakdown may be very different than this as to allotment of time, after all this person is a unique individual. I offer this to you simply as a device to help you stay within the constraints of time.

Take your material and sort it into categories. This can be easily accomplished (keep an eye on your master list). Take a coloured felt pen (so the numbers stand out). Take all your information, one piece of paper at a time, place the appropriate number on that paper identifying it's category (information on person's history, No. 2, a fact about his volunteerism, No. 5, a comment from one of his co-workers, No. 6, a comment your not sure of, No. 10). If you have three different categories on one page, take scissors and cut them apart, number them and place on appropriate pile. After you have finished this exercise you should be left with about 8 to 10 piles of paper in a semi-circle within easy reach.

If you have decided to use a special theme or inner passion (Chapter III - Special , Page 24) it may be appropriate to place it on your master list now.

The next step is to begin to build your talk. Go to Pile No. 1, Opening, where the best ideas will literally jump out at you. Write these on the master list right away, while others will be easily discarded, or placed on a separate pile. Some you are unsure of, leave them there, and some you know are good ideas but should be reclassified - numbered different or put in General Pile No. 10. Revisit this process as many times as necessary. It may be up to four or five times, every time adding portions and ideas and phrases to the structure of this category. Once you feel you are 95% complete in this area, move on to number two and so on till complete. Another idea you may want to use is to highlight a discarded idea or portion of one so it doesn't find it's way back again with useable ideas.

Ideas are like nature, like a farmer's seed, you see one and they proliferate or encourage others. Once you go through this process, you see that the hard work is paying off as the most worthwhile treasure, the finest gems are brought to the surface.

Now if you run into an impasse and you need more information, refer back to your General Information Pile No 10. It will jog your thought process and get you going again. As you are doing this, take a break, at least every hour. Once complete in rough, go back and complete the details, polish it up and get it to where you are satisfied. I have found that for every minute I speak I require about one hour of preparation time that includes material gathering, categorizing and practising the talk for delivery. This, I am sure, varies as to individuals depending on experience, etc.

So that you might be better able to see how this master list works, let's look at an actual example. The lady in question, Virginia Curtis, a mother of two, died at the age of forty-nine years after a valiant battle with cancer. She and her husband, Bill were very dear friends of mine.

Did I want to write a loving, passionate eulogy for them? You bet! (Her eulogy is found on Page 78. The following includes excerpts only.)

Master List
(remember this is a guide, it is not set in stone)

For: Mrs. Virginia Curtis

Special Theme: Artistic ability, others I have used cooking, faith, kindness, essence of life, inner passion. This is simply a thread that helps to sew the coat of life together.

No. 1 - Opening

"Bill Sr., Billy Jr., David & Kirsten, family, Rev. Rick Brown and friends of Virginia. Virginia Curtis was many things to many people...a wife, a mother, a loving friend and confidante. In whatever capacity we knew her we knew her to be gentle, warm, loving, caring, non-judgmental and humble."

_____

_____

_____

_____

No. 1 - Opening
ie: Salutation to spouse, children, friend, clergy, etc.

Other potential openings:

-bible verse
-history - start with day born
-go right into some of their finest characteristics
-customize it to this individual
-remember the order of these categories, 1 - 10, can
be interchanged without any impact on the outcome
-this information comes from Pile No. 1

If you have trouble organizing a certain category, don't
hesitate to make up a master list for that category. This
will provide you with more avenues to place ideas on, after
all ideas are the greatest wealth in the world.

No.2 History

"Virginia Curtis was born in Medicine Hat, Alberta on
September 30, 1947 to Elvina and Albert Krauss, she has a
brother Greg and a sister Sylvia. While working at the Bank
of Commerce she met her future life's partner, Bill Sr., they
were married on August 6, 1966. They were blessed with
two boys, Bill Jr. and David and have lately added a daughter-in-law, Kristen, wife of David. These two boys quickly
became the heart and soul, the substance of Virginia and
Bill's existence."

_____

_____

_____

_____

_____

_____

_____

_____

This particular information would come from data provided by the family in filling out History Questionnaire, Page
6. This category can vary greatly in size depending on detail you and the family want to use. This information comes
from Information Pile No. 2.

No. 3 Family

" Family embossed in gold, was the pride of that landscape and one of the most beautiful parts of her canvass.
Virginia and Bill have proudly raised two confident, mature, optimistic, loving individuals. This is a testimonial to
their dedication and determination. Virginia was so proud
of her two boys, Billy and David and her new daughter-in-
law, Kristen. She loved you all unconditionally and she
praised you at every opportunity. Bill Sr. said they couldn't
of had a better Mother."

_____

_____

_____

_____

_____

_____

_____

Notes: Here utilize information gained from Family Questionnaire Page 9. Anything relating to family can be used in this category. You could possibly use a family story or add material as it relates to family ties, relationships, etc. (loving, warm, humorous, positive, direct quotes from grandchildren or family members can add a lot). Information for this category comes from Pile 3.

No. 4 Friends

"A major part of this divine portrait of Virginia was the word friendship. Punctuality as many of you knew was not a strong suit for Virginia, but probably for good reason. No matter how busy she was, she always made time for her friends. For many to have one true friend in life is a treasure, but the fact Virginia had so many genuine, sincere, loving friends is proof of a great person. Some of her friends comments about her included, never thinks of herself, listens, sensitive, sincere, really cares, optimistic, positive, always places others needs before her own, makes us feel special, never said an unkind word about anyone, and would do anything for us."

_____

_____

_____

_____

_____

_____

_____

Notes: Use results from Friends Questionnaire, Page 11 to fill category No. 4. Direct quotes from friends also can be productive here if you are short on words. Use Descriptive Words, Chapter IV, Page 28. Use information Pile 4.

No. 5 Volunteerism - Community Involvement

"The Good Lord must have had trouble painting Virginia, wouldn't you agree, because she never sat around long enough for that to happen. She was always on the move, always doing for someone else. She raised money for M.S. through cycling 100 km, winning the top prize one year, volunteered for Victim Services, visited shut-ins, loved to work for Mom of Pre-Schoolers, loved to teach youngsters about art, and was involved in the art club and Anglican Church. The most important quality was that she was a great neighbour, acting as a second mom to all the neighbourhood kids, a Block Parent before the word was invented. The Curtis Family opened a major recreation area in Westlock in their back yard by investing in a trampoline. Virginia gave freely of hospitality, hugs, cookies, food, first aid, kindness, respect and love. The Curtis home was a beehive of activity. It was a selfless home where no one was turned away. The door was never locked and her heart was always open.

Note: Many people are proud of their community involvement, so this is a good area to concentrate on. Take information for this from all areas but especially Volunteer Questionnaire, Page 13 and of course from Information Pile 5.

No. 6 Profession /Career

" Virginia's art and sign work were known throughout the community as first class. She had an eye for visualization like I have never seen before. If you gave her a concept she quickly turned it into something concrete that was far beyond what you had ever expected. Many times I would go to her shop perfectly satisfied with the work she had done, yet Virginia would not let it go because it didn't meet her own high standard."

_____

_____

_____

_____

_____

_____

Notes: Use information from Pile No. 6 and information from Profession-Career Questionnaire, Page 14.

No. 7 Hobbies

"Virginia did not have a lot of hobbies but she enjoyed travelling with her boys to sporting events." In a case like this I used this extra time in my eulogy to concentrate on an area Virginia had lot of depth in. For someone else hobbies may take 100-150 words which goes to prove people are different and thank God they are.

_____

_____

_____

_____

_____

Notes: Information comes from Hobbies Questionnaire, Pile 7, Page 16.

No. 8 Praise

"So what is this essence of life that sets Virginia, this masterpiece, apart from so many others. Could it be the unique and profound snow white colour of faith. To Virginia faith was unshakeable, immovable. It's ironic isn't it, November 11 is today, Remembrance Day, symbolic of courage, of bravery, of steadfastness, like an oak tree. Such was the nature of Virginia's faith as she confronted this wicked disease. Always positive, never hateful, never complaining, never wanting to upset, never wanting to worry, never wanting to bother.

Virginia's talented brush of life has touched so many of us, it lives on through her beautiful signs, her loving family. It lives on through the loyalty and devotion of her friends."

Notes: To me this is the category where the finest kernels, the most extraordinary jewels are found. It is here you want to praise in an inspired and impassioned way using the vitality and excitement only enthusiasm and hard work can provide. Information comes from Pile No. 8, Praise Questionnaire, Page 17.

No. 9 Close

" In closing maybe the best we could do is continue to paint some pictures in her memory, in her honour. Open your home to a neighbourhood child, visit a shut-in (as Virginia did on a regular basis), extend friendship to someone new, love your spouse more, love your children more. We say goodbye to you now, Virginia as you take your rightful place with the Master Artist himself in his Heavenly Art Gallery."

_____

_____

_____

_____

_____

_____

_____

_____

Notes: The close is like a goodbye, some I have seen ended with a poem, song or challenge to keep them alive with an act of good. Use information here from Pile No. 9. Don't hesitate to put your own autographed idea into this area.

In this example I relate to a special theme, which in the case of Mrs. Curtis was her artistic ability. I used this as a thread, as a common denominator producing a compelling portrait of a beautiful person. I hope you can use this technique; it appears to add to the end product. If you have information left over plus your rough notes, don't throw them away as you may be asked again and this will be a tremendous resource. If you just have your talk in rough as this area comes to a conclusion, you may want to finalize the full discourse. If you are circulating copies, edit the final copy.

Take a break you deserve it. Pat yourself on the back.

CHAPTER VI

WRAPPING THE GIFT

CHAPTER VI

WRAPPING THE GIFT

Well it's taken a lot of work, but your hand made gift is complete and if your at this point in the book you've no doubt done an admirable job. So what do you do now with a magnificent legacy of this nature, as you get ready to transport it? You wrap it of course, but not with just any old gift wrap laying around the house. You utilize the remarkable, colourful, caring wrap of capable public speaking; you fasten it with the sturdy, reliable ribbon of diligent and determined practice, and finally to top it all off, you use the bright vital bow of an impassioned delivery system.

It is said that one of the most important skills in life that will help you succeed is the ability to communicate, to speak in public. This ability will yield self confidence, positive self esteem and the ability to reason. Let's look at this vehicle we call public speaking. It is a critical element because it will allow us to transport our wondrous gift safely and carefully to its rightful destination.

Every good speaker is nervous. It's natural and normal. It allows you to perform at your peak ability. The key is to harness it, control it, put it to work for you. It's called getting the butterflies, to fly in formation, and there are many ways to do it.

You have already put together an outstanding well prepared talk and this is a tremendous confidence boost. Learn a delivery system; reading, cue cards and key words or no written notes. Once you have chosen a delivery system, practice, practice, then practice some more. They would never let you drive without practising. Really for any activity in life you want to excel in, you have to pay the price.

Public speaking is like that. It requires some effort and time. The wonderful by-product is that it creates confidence which in turn creates a relaxed atmosphere.

There are two additional ways to practice that can also be very valuable. One is to go to the actual facility you will be doing your presentation at and go through the same detailed steps you will do when you are actually delivering it. Sit where you will sit, walk the route you will take. If there is a microphone system, turn it on, adjust it to your height. Test it about 8 - 10" away. If using notes take them out, if there is no podium, hold them at a comfortable distance, not too low so you can't see or to high as to hide your face. Look out in the audience, establish your presence, give a warm, kind, caring, genuine smile. Begin your talk at the same voice speed you normally use. Visualize the audience, the people in their seats, as much detail as possible. If you can't go to the facility, do this at home. This is a tremendous confidence lifter and when you actually do it, it will seem like a simple repetition.

A second way is to practice in front of a small group of friends and family. Go through the exact talk just like you intend to deliver it. As you go through this, you may notice some sentence structures or words that don't feel right. Make mental notes of them and after you have finished your discourse, edit them. Whenever possible, practice saying it out loud, as the feedback of your actual voice is very reassuring and will aid in creating extra confidence.

This may be one of the most important points in this book, it is one of the great unwritten Laws of Life. Focus on others relieves pressure on you. In my own experience, the best way to control a fuse burning out in a car is to insure you don't overburden one specific circuit. The same falls true in delivering a eulogy. How do you do this? It's easy. Concentrate on placing the concerns of others before your very own. Let's face it, this is probably one of the worst weeks in these peoples lives; they have lost a loved one. So don't worry about your own performance (if well prepared and practised you will do fine). Focus some of your time on lightening their load in any way possible. I remember when

I did my own Father-in-law's eulogy. I was so worried, so wound up about my personal effort or offering, my own self doubts, I had forgotten to worry about my wife, her family, their feelings, their sense of loss. As soon as I immersed myself in sincerely helping them get through this most difficult time in their lives, it was like a miracle. My part, the eulogy, went off without a hitch.

So lighten their load in any way possible. It may be a ride, a hug, a kind word and of course, the giving of a beautiful gift of comfort and love, the eulogy. This approach is one of the most wonderful things you can do. You lighten someone else's load and you also lighten your own. It will relax you and take away some of your anxiety, after all, "Fear Inhibits, Love Enhances."

Let's take a moment now to talk about some of the key elements of Public Speaking:

-People expect sincerity, not high oratory. People are pulling for you because of the solemnity of the occasion. Remember the focus is not on the messenger but on the message.

-If you are a bit nervous or you mispronounce a word, don't hesitate or apologize. It probably wasn't noticed and apologizing just puts you off track and may cause you to lose some of your confidence. Just forge ahead and do the wonderful job you're capable of.

-Eye contact is one of the most important aspects of public speaking, so use as much eye contact as possible. It is a by-product of sound preparation. It allows you to visit, to scan all parts of the room, to hold the audience's attention as you present your material in a cup of coffee conversational type fashion. The only caveat I have on eye contact is my own particular affliction, I am very emotional, especially if I see people crying or suffering. If you are also of this nature, you may want to avoid direct eye contact with family members or close friends seated at the front of the room. This can be accomplished by using eye contact with the back 80% of the room.

-Make sure that you make effective use of the microphone. I recall going to a School Graduation where it was very evident that one of the young presenters had spent a great deal of time preparing a talk, but no one heard it. She stood too far from the mike. Before people arrive check that the mike is on and working and if necessary have them turn it up. Speak about 10" away from the mike and directly into it. Be careful not to turn your head too far away from it as it may not pick up your voice. If working properly you can hear the strength level of your message coming back to you. Even if you have a mike you still have to speak clearly and loudly. Take your time between sentences and don't be scared to repeat an important part. This all helps in having your message heard, after all no matter how good it is if they can't hear it, it won't be of benefit to anyone.

If the microphone has too much static or breaks down during your presentation shut it off. Speak as loudly as you can because even in a very large room, if the audience is quiet, your voice will carry a long way. While on this subject, if for some unusual reason a distraction comes up like a train going by, a baby crying, or a major air conditioner comes on, just stop until the train goes by so to speak. People want to hear the message - don't deny them that opportunity.

-Proper speaking posture is important. Stand straight, one foot slightly ahead of the other. This allows you to move a slight bit, serving to keep you at ease. Don't lean on podium or lectern, remain independent from these structures. Don't anchor your hands on lectern, it just gives you a rigid unnatural appearance.

-This leads us into another very important aspect of public speaking. It is used to direct, to help convey our message, our intent to those around us. These are called gestures, facial and hand, the unofficial language of the body. This is why in the previous point I mentioned not to latch on to the podium. When your hands are free it allows them to operate in a natural unencumbered fashion.

In some schools of thought relating to public speaking

they have a complete detailed system of encouraging gestures. In my mind, I suggest you not pursue this avenue. Gestures are natural and are most effective when left to develop on their own. So just forget about them, they, if unimpeded, will flourish on their own. If you have no podium and your hands do feel uncomfortable, a possible solution is to hold on to your notes or place one hand inside the other. This   gives you the potential of unrestricted movement.

-Use your normal voice speed as there is a tendency in public speaking to talk faster than usual - avoid this trap. Pronounce carefully and even a little slower than normal. Let your voice show your emotion, your sincerity in being chosen spokesman for this entire group. Vary your tempo and rate of delivery and show some voice modulation. If you want to pay particular attention to a certain segment of your talk, don't be afraid to repeat it. A friendly relaxed discussional tone is the most pleasant to listen to.

-Enthusiasm can add a lot, but what is this enthusiasm? Enthusiasm is a person's deep desire to convey a message from their heart and soul and mind to the heart and soul and mind of their audience in a sincere, vital, and fervent way. You've heard this before in this book, but I repeat it because it is so important. You do this by bringing those words to life through yourself, always guiding, always inspiring, always encouraging by giving the greatest gift on earth, a gift of yourself, for the benefit of others!

-Use great care in grooming and clothes; neat and tidy are our goals. For men, I suggest a suit and tie, sweater and tie (quiet tie), dress pants (avoid loud colours). Women should wear , a dress suit, jacket with dress, modest length, subtle colours, avoiding excessive perfume and makeup. In general, wear clean clothes that are well pressed, socks or hose with no holes and comfortable shoes that have been polished. Avoid heavy clothes, think cool. Get clothes ready the day before taking an extra worry out of the way. Look good! Feel good! Do Good!

Now we have this finely tuned, well oiled machine of

public speaking ready to go. So which highway do we want to travel on to deliver our gift. We've got three major choices, the secondary highway - reading, the two lane of key words or the divided highway of no written notes. Any of these will get you to your destination safe and sound. Which should you choose. This will depend entirely on two things. One, how much time you have to prepare and secondly the amount of experience you have, but no matter which one you do choose all the parts of our public speaking vehicle apply. So let's take a look at the descriptive literature on these three different roads.

Now the secondary highway of reading is a good one but it is more bumpy, more complicated than first meets the eye. I am sure you've attended a function when somebody read their presentation, reading it so poorly that it was as exciting as watching paint dry. It can also be a great cure for insomnia, but if done properly and using proper techniques it can end up being exceptional. Insure your notes are written neatly or typed on cue cards about 5" x 6" so they can fit in your suit or purse. Number them in case they get out of order. The reason I discourage full sized sheets of paper is if you don't have the benefit of a podium they may end up shaking or fluttering. This has the effect of distracting both the audience and yourself.

Now you may wonder when a politician is giving a long discourse how they manage to look up about half the time, thus salvaging one their most important attributes, eye contact. What they do is slowly read the sentence, take a word picture of the final half of the sentence, look up and repeat it. They get so adept at this that they can go on for quite a few words. As they practice (you may want to do this) they many even underline or put in bold letters when and where they will look up. If you choose to use this system it may be advisable to place your finger where you will stop to insure you don't lose your place. This system still requires a substantial amount of practice to insure proper pronunciation, timing and the use of as much eye contact as possible.

A large number of people may choose this system in the case of a eulogy, because you have little time to prepare. In addition, if you have little or no experience public speaking, you should probably take this route and challenge yourself to travel the other highways in the near future as you undertake other public speaking duties.

The second selection available to you is the two lane highway of key words. In this application you also use numbered cue cards, using the text of your full discourse reading it over several times. Through the course of this process pick out a memorable word, a key word or phrase that will jog your memory into recalling the whole paragraph. Write these items on a cue card in bold large letters in the order that they will appear, doing the whole talk in this fashion. Again read it several times making mental associations with your key words or key phrases.

Then start to practice it out loud, be careful not to memorize it, just familiarize it. The dangerous part of memorizing of course is if you miss one word, it may be very difficult for you to get started again. A memorized talk is devoid of any sincerity or emotion.

If you are doing it correctly, just holding your cue cards and taking guidance from just those words, you will find your talk will be a little different every time you say it. This is good because the effect will be a natural conversational type of effort. So by all means, you a more experienced speaker will want to take advantage of increased eye contact, utilize this thoroughfare.

Our third choice is the four lane of no written notes, notice the no, there are notes of course, but they are not written ones. I am sure you've been to a gathering, a meeting and observed a speaker go up and talk for half an hour or more and not visibly use any notes, and you maybe said to yourself, "isn't that amazing, I wish I could do that. Well I am here to tell you that you can, and it's easy!

Now that amazing speaker we just talked about, did have notes, in fact detailed notes stored in his head. You would never take off on a long voyage without a detailed map and no experienced speaker would either.

It's been proven that we can recall an amazing number of items, if we associate them with something else, and paint a word picture of this association. Okay, let's do one, so you can see what I mean! Refer to eulogy, Virginia Curtis, Page 78. On this highway we use letters of the alphabet as sign markers to use as concrete reference points (detailed map) to guide us and help us from getting lost.

Here is what I mean:

A = A Frame Cabin
B = Body - Muscular
C = Couch
D = Dog
E = Elephant
F = Fireplace
G
H
I

Use as many as you require, you can use the whole alphabet. For a ten to twelve minute talk, ten letters will usually be more than ample. Use your own word pictures, something that starts with the same letter of the alphabet so it stays in order in your mind.

As I prepare a talk, I begin by focusing very clearly in my mind on A Frame Cabin (I owned one). On the front of the cabin are two large green planters, here on the left I start my talk, my opening, by having the people who I will address sit on it in the order I will name them ie. her husband, Bill Sr., son Billy Jr., son David and daughter-in-law Kristen, and on the other planter, a large group of her friends. Then above the planter fastened to the window I have a cute huggable teddy bear, with a love heart on its chest. This will give me the idea about Virginia being a warm loving and caring person. Then in the other window I will have dangling a spool of red thread with a paper marked, humble, attached to it, this will give me the information I need to relate the ideas about Virginia as a person, woven from the strands of service to others above self.

I see right on the peak of the A frame, a medicine man to represent the City of Medicine Hat, Alberta (her birthplace) and written on his chest is September 30, 1947 (her birth date). He is holding by one hand her parents, Elvina and Albert Kraus and the other hand her brother and sister Greg and Sylvia.

Attached to one eave is a picture of the bank where she worked with her future husband. I see Bill walking through the front door dressed in his wedding suit and on the other side of the eave sliding off the roof are her two boys, Billy and David and on the ground ready to break their fall are Bill Sr. and Virginia. This represents the fact they are so important and they at birth quickly became the centre of their life.

Then I would move to the B (if you use this system often enough these word pictures become like second nature) Here my picture is of a Olympic body builder. I can see him now and in his right hand, he would hold a vision of Virginia standing behind an easel painting a beautiful portrait, this reminds me easily of her artistic ability, then let's move to the left hand, his left shoulder, top of his head, other shoulder, his right foot, left foot, his belt buckle. I could use him as a bulletin board for three to nine paragraphs. See what we've done, we've created a highway which you follow in standard order and the beauty of this highway is it doesn't have ditches to fall into, you just follow it, not turning off. When you work on this system for a few hours, leave it to come back, say the next day, you will easily forget the ideas, but you won't forget the word associations. Easy, isn't it, and it works. I go through the whole talk like that and make word pictures for every paragraph. Even in Virginia's whole eulogy it only took me about eight to nine word pictures to complete the whole talk by simply following the letters of the alphabet like a road map. You virtually can't miss anything. But if you get lost, the important thing to remember is don't panic, just keep talking, filling in with related material. After all, they don't know the road, they don't know you're lost.

I recall one occasion when I had just been public speaking for a short while using this system. While speaking in front of about five hundred people I lost my train of thought. So what do you do. You quickly send out a search party, yes, that's right, right inside your head. Oh let's see where was I, oh yes, just starting on the idea located on the trunk of the elephant, you see the trunk, you see the idea and away you go again, no one the wiser.

This system works and it works well, try it, to remember names. The gentlemen's name is Lyons, portray him as having a lion's head, I bet you will never forget it. Try it when your spouse tells you to pick up ten items at the store, try it without paper. You will be amazed and your spouse will be too, when you come home with all the items. After all, how could you forget a cornflakes box resting on the back of an elephant.

Try it when listening to a speaker when you don't have pen and paper and you want to remember five or six of the main points. Use your pictorial road map, it's so effective.

The advantages of this system in delivering a talk are obvious. The most important is constant and undisturbed eye contact resulting in increased audience attention. This allows you to concentrate on giving the talk heart to heart, instead of fumbling or being distracted by written notes. Hey! These notes, you can't lose them, and nobody can steal them! So, should you use this system if you are only just getting started in public speaking, not likely. Public speaking is like any other learning process, it's learned a little bit at a time in a progressive step by step fashion. However, I would hasten to encourage you to try it on a two or three minute presentation then later a five minute one and so on as your confidence builds. This highway once learned is the easiest to drive, yes it is indeed an impressive highway.

When you use this system, just like the two lane highway, you will find that every time you use it, it will turn out a bit different. This is good and indicates you aren't stuck on any specific words and that you've resisted the temptation to memorize. Another good thing about no written notes is you can practice this talk in the car, while you wait for the dentist, wherever!

If this type of information interests you it may be advisable for you to take a public speaking course, there are a lot of good ones around.

Before I leave this area of our journey I want to encourage you that whatever highway you choose to travel, practice that route over and over again. No, I'm not a task master, this notion is born from my sincere desire to see you do well. It's almost like a math formula when you think about it:

MT = CAR

More Time = Confidence Assurance and Relaxation. The more time spent practising the more car you will have!

So we've come to a conclusion in this very important chapter. We are also getting very close to the end of our overall journey. Let me again congratulate you at this juncture in the book for your diligence and hard work! So where do we find ourselves now; let's take inventory. We've got a brand new shiny, very articulate gift, wrapped nicely in public speaking ability, with every detail practised. What's this inventory taking tell us. It tells us success can't be to far away!

CHAPTER VII

THE DELIVERY

CHAPTER VII

THE DELIVERY

O kay, today is the magnificent day we deliver our gift, and in some ways it's similar to delivering a baby. You can easily compare the eulogist to an expectant mother, you both are anxious to see what this wondrous masterpiece looks like at full maturity. You both know from first hand experience the tremendous effort, sacrifice and love that has gone into the preparation for this big day. You both are individuals who have placed the concern of others before your own, and like my beautiful wife Bonnie has told me, once it's over, it's over, all is forgotten and only the amazement, happiness, joy and wonder of new life is remembered.

So we've got a beautiful gift to deliver, we're well prepared, well organized and we're taking the reliable vehicle of public speaking in preparation of travelling on a terrific highway. Before we leave, let's make sure we've packed all that we are going to require:

1. Insure you get up early, you don't want to rush. Give yourself lots of time and before you have breakfast, practice your talk several times. Visualize yourself at the podium doing an inspired job, see yourself calm and confident. If a word or phrase still feels uncomfortable it's not too late to change it. However resist any temptation to make major changes.

2. This is one of the most important parts of yours day's preparation. Insist mentally to yourself that you focus on others. It's time to recall the stress and tremendous load the family and friends have been under during the past few days. Recall to yourself that this is the reason

that you have built with your own hands, this remark-able gift. You hope in some small way that this gift will alleviate some of their pain and suffering.

3. Try as much as possible to delegate or postpone any other responsibilities you have today, so that you might concentrate on the job at hand.

4. After practising, attend to other details of preparation, break-fast, clothing, hair, etc.

5. Maybe about 90 minutes before you leave, have a hot bath and practice your whole talk again (careful you don't wet your notes, always have another copy in case). I don't know if this is for you, but I find this very relaxing, private and quiet.

6. Recheck the time of the service. Ensure you allow plenty of time to get there 30 to 40 minutes before the start (especially if you haven't been there before).

7. Final Checklist - before leaving:

   -look in mirror to check clothes, hair, overall appearance - neat and tidy.
   -need a comb or brush (maybe windy).
   -Kleenex.
   -map and address of facility.
   -breath candy (mouth gets dry-required for before and after, have it in pocket for easy access - do not go to po-dium with candy or gum in mouth).
   -your notes in numbered order, held together with small clamp. Insure you place it in pocket of suit or purse.
   -leave early - give yourself lots of time.
   -Look Good! Feel Good! Do Good!

8. Try to get someone else to drive as you have enough on your mind. If this is the case, as you go along, again review your talk. However, if you are driving, concentrate on the road, I want you to get there safe!

9. Checklist upon arrival at facility - time will move quickly, so get about your duties:

-check your coat, ensure you have your notes with you, go to the bathroom, check hair, clothes, overall appearance, breath candy. At this point, don't think of the eulogy itself, attend to other details.

-go to the Minister or Clergyman - quickly again review place and time in service where you are going to make your presentation. Ask where he or she would like you to sit or any other instructions they would like to give you.

-check microphone system, insure you know how to turn it on and how to adjust it. If you feel it is not loud enough, ask the facility operator if they would mind if you turned it up. Better now than during the service.

-check podium to see how it will adjust, relate to the usage of your notes. Ensure there is easy access, watch for cords or other walking impediments. Sit within easy walking distance from the podium or lectern.

-speak to the undertaker, tell them you are the eulogist, do they have any instruction for you. Leave extra copies of eulogy (if family requested) with undertaker for distribution after the service.

-again focus on family members that may need a word of encouragement or a hug. For the moment place all your attention on them. Ask if there are any last minute instructions they may want you to add. Adjust your notes accordingly. This shows dignity and respect for all concerned.

-ten or fifteen minutes before the service starts, go to your seat, it maybe the opportune time here to take a final peak at the gift. In many cases if people know you are giving the eulogy they may look at you a bit more than normal. No matter how you are feeling, react with a calm relaxed appearance, after all we know they are all pulling for you to do well.

-service starts, you are about three - four minutes away

from going up. Feel the confidence grow in you now as you think how well prepared you are, about the extensive material you've gathered and how well organized it is. To top all this off, it's been very well rehearsed.

I played hockey for thirty-five years and without fail, before every game I felt a tinge of anxiety. This is wonderful because it's your body's way of telling you it's ready to support you in every way possible.

As the final moment approaches, again, focus your mind on the privilege of helping these people. That this gift is entirely for them with no strings attached, with no thought for recompense, and that you hope in some small way it will lessen their grief. If you feel a bit anxious, here is a little tip for you. Intense physical pressure of sorts seems to drain excess energy and anxiety away from you. Here's what I mean. Take both hands (no one will see this) and press as hard as you can against the outside of your knee (towards the middle). Let your knees exert pressure to the outside to resist this pressure. Do this several times and a good part of your anxiety should be relieved.

The Minister is motioning to you, it is time, walk confidently and slowly to the podium, take charge of the situation as you look over the audience, give a warm loving smile, adjust the mike if necessary. It's time to unwrap the gift. Begin slowly and present your talk exactly as you practised it, in a fluent sincere way. Put meaning in every word, pause between paragraphs, use as much eye contact as possible but most important of all use your public speaking vehicle as you drive this gift proudly and humbly to its successful conclusion.

During the course of your talk a little voice in your head will tell you well done, this is going pretty well. People may not be able to see all the work that went into your eulogy but they will sense the care and trouble you went through. Some will tell you that you made that look easy, that you looked very relaxed - well we know different, don't we.

Well the birth is over and we revel in the new life. This

Eulogy may very well be the spark that will allow this individual to live on in the hearts and minds and memory of family and friends. A tremendous sense of pride and accomplishment will be walking partners with you as you return to your seat.

At the lunch afterwards many people will compliment you for your inspired and amazing gift. It may be one of the greatest accomplishments of your life. After all you exposed yourself, you took a risk to help family and friends feel good about yourself - you deserve it.

How do you react to these compliments? I would think a short humble response is most appropriate - Thank you very much. Well I was fortunate, I had a wonderful subject, etc.

In coming to a close my deepest desire, my most sincere hope is that in some small way I have helped you. Like the kindergarten child, to build a gift with your own loving hands and your own selfless spirit, a gift of love to family and friends.

I would like to ask you one last favour my friend, to pass this gift on, share your eulogy with others, to coach others, to allow it simply to touch someone else's life. By the way, keep all your rough notes, you may be required to do it again!

We will be adding a second volume in the near future. We would love to hear from you on your experience. Please send us a copy of your eulogy for possible inclusion in our next edition. If you have any suggestions or feedback please forward it to me at:

Leo Seguin
10712 - 101 Street
Westlock, Alberta, Canada
T7P 1H7
Telephone: (780) 349-3300
Fax: (780) 349-6301
Toll Free: 1-877-460-0053
Email: eulogy@telusplanet.net

CHAPTER VIII

ACTUAL
EULOGIES

CHAPTER VIII

ACTUAL EULOGIES

GARRY NELSON

JANUARY 3, 1954 - JUNE 3, 1989

WRITTEN BY PENNY BILODEAU AND RYAN MANTON

DELIVERED BY RYAN MANTON

I remember Garry Nelson. When I think of him, a smile bright as ever is what I'm really thinking about. A beaming smile with a stem from a radiant heart, longing to share with friends and people alike, an abundance of simple happiness stored inside. My friends, we have a mighty big task in front of us, if we want to continue in the path of the spirit Garry laid the ground work for and blazed all of his thirty-five years on this earth. A big task indeed. And when I think back, it's been a short thirty-five years.

My recollection of our friendship starts in high school. You know, the days of pimples and peer pressure. Even then, however, I remember the radiant fellowship flowing through. The uncanny ability to make his fellow students howl with laughter. A trait that few of us have really mastered genuinely. But with Garry, he had mastered it. And with Garry it was genuine.

I remember a couple of times giving him a ride home to Clyde on my motorcycle. He did love that bike. And it was one of these times between Westlock and Clyde that I distinctly remember wondering whether it was the wind making my eyes water or if it was just Garry being so extremely funny as to bring tears to my eyes with laughter. I distinctly recall him expressing his opinion of the opposite gender. That conversation must have lingered, as he and I remained bachelors. I wish that I could have gone to school with him all the way through from grade one. However, he grew up in Clyde and I grew up in Westlock. He took his elementary and primary schooling in Edmonton and Clyde and came over to Westlock in Grade Ten. I remember us both on the same basketball team. Mutt and Jeff we were. As I look back, we thought we were doing good, but really I think we were only just putting in time. Garry wasn't tall in high school but blossomed, so to speak and grew tall after high school. Nevertheless, he loved most sports and still played basketball.

Some people are often the object of laughter, but that's a different kind of humour. The humour that comes from the minds and mouths of insensitive and uncaring youth. The kind of humour that's not from the heart but from untalented wit. Not so with Garry. His humour was gifted. I recall the retaliatory remarks in school made by him to any slander. I think, with a quick-witted, double-edged reply that he always emitted from his heart. Putting the guy in his place, but never being cruel. Garry was not a cruel man.

Very few people knew that as an infant, he had a very lengthy illness of pneumonia and bronchitis that weakened and hospitalized him off and on for better than a year and a half. In later years he had trouble with his legs. So if his jump shots on basketball teams weren't all that spectacular, perhaps he had just cause.

After graduation, he took a chef's course at N.A.I.T. the next year in 1972. I guess he decided that shift work as a chef interrupted his social life, so he tried different things in life throughout the years. I remember he always said he could always fall back on his chef training. I understand though, that he did show many people how to carve a turkey properly. To show his determination, however, Garry chose a career in his last years that took him to great heights, so to speak. Those same legs that might not have been so swift on the basketball court were steady as a rock as he climbed microwave and other towers sever hundred feet high in and around western and northern Canada. Surrounded by constant danger in this job, I'm sure Garry did his work with a smile. I'm also sure he was respected by his fellow colleagues.

Garry not only had the gift of humouring people with good jokes but often played jokes on people. Penny's Christmas gift one year from Garry was a gift that he took great pains in camouflaging. Putting it inside a ball glove, he wrapped the glove with several rolls of electricians tape. Just to get her goat, I guess. It took her a long time, needless to say, to open the gift.

I wonder if his niece and nephew knew how much he loved them. He's always talked to me about them as if they were his own. I guess he never had children of his own so they were like his. He always reminded Brandi, for instance, to keep her judo moves in tournament play and on the practice floor and not use them on him. I can see him saying that too. He called her the 'trained killer'. She is proficient in judo. I'm sure his love of hockey never ended with watching his nephew Brent play the game. He also played hockey himself. I never had the opportunity to watch Garry actually play hockey but I'm sure that it would have been entertaining. I did know him when he was emphatically involved with the local Westlock Wolves hockey club. A more dedicated assistant and fan I have never known, you could always hear Garry head and shoulders above the rest of the crowd. It not yelling encouragement to his team, hassling the ref, I'm sure, into early retirement. He'd come into our store, I remember, the next day so hoarse that he could hardly talk.

He did have his serious side too and was always in tune to the hearts and wants and needs of his fellow man. For instance, he had an unusual blood type. The Red Cross was always after him for donations of his blood. A rare Blood. He gave endlessly. Garry took time to visit with young and old alike. He kept in touch with family and friends always. He'd call his family from way north in the Northwest Territories at all times of the day or night. Just to talk. He was a benevolent person. He always gave to Santas' Anonymous and he played his part in getting toys to people that deserved them. Children especially.

He never forgot birthdays or anniversaries. He was always punctual. An attribute, just in itself, to be commended. He was an accurate man. He was very neat. His personal effects were always in order. Meticulously arranged. I never saw Garry in a shabby state of dress or cleanliness. Even when he strolled through the door of our store in a big Stetson and cowboy boots, he always looked good and still looked good. Everything just like new.

Yes, Garry was a fan of rodeos and attended, even helping out at several of the events in the seventies and early eighties. He had a soft spot for animals as well. Garry loved to dance and attended occasions where he could be among people and could share laughter and make them laugh. Actually people loved being around Garry as well. They attended a function and if he was there, then there was never a dull moment. I remember going to a wedding and a dance with Garry and friends and remember being entertained the whole evening through by this man. I love to dance too but I was content to just spend time with Garry and enjoy in joking and laughing.

I have something here given to me by his working colleagues that he would like me to read:

Garry worked with the Transport Canada steel crew the past seven years. His passing was a great loss to all of us. Most of the steel crew, except for Jack and Rick, can not be here today. They are in northern B.C. on a job and I'm sure Garry will understand the circumstances. There is a large representation from Transport Canada here, however, and that's good to see. Garry, whether it be work or just everyday life, lived each day the same. With pride, dedication, humour and concern for his fellow workers, family and friends. On behalf of the steel crew and the 'Falcons' hockey team, Garry will be sadly missed. I'm also told that in memory of Garry, his fellow players are seeing that an annual tournament is named after him.

I'm sure Garry was proud of the fact he was the oldest grandson of twenty-six grandchildren. I know that the Nelson family - Brad, Penny, Laverne and Stan, have a wonderful outlook on life. One of joyfulness and pleasantness. They have the attributes that Garry was the epitome of. It has been a pleasure and an honour knowing Garry and his family, as they have all touched my heart. You ought to and I know you will carry on in his fashion I'm sure he would have us all live life.

I can't say goodbye to you Garry, because I know all I have to do is close my eyes and that smiling face will be right there. I'm sure those of us whose hearts have been touched by this man have that same felling. So why don't we all, from time to time, just close our eyes and say hello Garry.

HENRY LEON OKO

DECEMBER 3, 1921 - MARCH 31, 1985

WRITTEN AND DELIVERED BY LEO SEGUIN

Henry Leon Oko was born December the 3rd, 1921 in Tawatinaw, the youngest son of Peter and Julia Oko. He attended the Golden Sunset School in the same village and later went farming with his older brothers until the age of 27. In 1948 he went into the restaurant business with his brother Tony, a couple of years later became a grain buyer for Parrish & Heimbecker in Nestow. Around 1951, Henry was making many trips to Musidora to supposedly see Steve Lysakowski, Rose's brother, it soon became apparent he was becoming more fond of Rose, than Steve, so on August 9th, 1952 Henry married Rose Lysakowski who he loved and treated as a lady all of his life. They were blessed by four daughters, Bonnie, Melody, Joni and Lori.

In 1953 Henry started his long proud career with the

United Grain Growers as an agent in Tawatinaw, during this time Henry assumed his responsibilities well and soon built a reputation as a very honest hard working individual, both with the company and everyone in the community. During this time he also won many awards for the cleanest elevator in the area. I think Henry looked after the elevator and Rose has a hand in the upkeep of the office. I'm sure it's the only time an elevator office was graced with curtains and a rug at the door, the farmers would literally take their shoes off. This was typical of the way Henry treated his work, seriously and with a great deal of pride and dedication. He did this throughout his 25 plus years with the United Grain Growers and he carried it with him in his other occupations, selling Hail Insurance and as a Canola buyer.

Henry really enjoyed being involved in the community, his friendly manner, I'm sure set everyone at ease. He loved to dance and he was also especially fond of sports like curling, baseball and hockey - both as an organizer and participant in his earlier years and in recent years as a spectator, he was also a member of our local council of the Knights of Columbus.

You know folks, 16 years ago I travelled to Tawatinaw and entered for the first time the house of Henry Oko, I had a date with his daughter. That day, I met the kindest man I've ever known in my life. I was treated by Henry with respect, kindness and consideration, the same way he treated everyone he knew. I never heard him utter an unkind word to anyone (I don't think the man was capable of it). Yes, Henry was a very special person and it's been proven, in fact over the past 16 years, I've discussed the subject of Henry Oko with many people and do you know I've never heard anyone, not one, say anything bad about him!

Some people would pay millions to be loved and respected like Henry. Henry was rich in his own way, no he didn't have a diamond ring or a gold necklace but he did have a heart of gold that allowed him to be kind and gentle and loving, he lived by a very special rule, that was as crystal clear as a diamond, that rule was, "It is in giving that we receive", I don't know if he ever said that, but I do know one thing for sure, he lived it everyday of his life, from nursing a kitten who had broken it's leg back to health, to offering financial assistance in hard times, to taking a carload of kids to the Drive-In.

Henry Oko was always giving, he gave many gifts but primarily he gave of himself for the benefit of others, and people could sense this, especially the grandchildren for they were forever hugging him around the neck, telling him how much they loved him.

I guess Rose, summed it up best when she said we've lost the best daddy in the world. Folks, I think we can consider ourselves very fortunate because many people go through life never having had the opportunity of meeting a man like Henry, and one thing, at this moment that is very clear in my mind - God has to be good to have shared Henry with us!

MARIE JANE OKO

DECEMBER 13, 1918 - JANUARY 22, 1996

WRITTEN AND DELIVERED BY LEO SEGUIN

Marie Jane Oko, one of eight children, was born December 13, 1918, to Pearl and Michael Lysakowski of Musidora, Alberta. She is survived by two sisters, Helen Arechuk of Beauvallon and Rose Oko of Westlock, She was predeceased by her parents, her brothers, Peter, Nick, Louis and Steve, and one sister, Anne.

Marie attended Franko Public School which is presently located at the Ukrainian Cultural Heritage Village near Elk

Island Park, and later completed her education in a two room high school in Plain Lake and from the University of Life and University of Experience. She had an Honours Degree in service to others above self.

In July 1939, Marie moved to Edmonton and worked for Swift Packing Plant, Pavey Candy and MacDonald Consolidated until 1944, when she met and married Tony Oko. In 1945, Marie and Tony settled in Tawatinaw and for 22 years they operated a restaurant and then a grocery store. In 1964 Marie accepted the position of local post mistress and worked until her retirement in 1971. At this time Marie and Tony moved to Westlock, where Marie catered to various social functions and was also employed by the Federal Government as a matron for the R.C.M.P. Tony passed away September 14, 1981.

Marie and Tony did their utmost to give their four children- Bob, Zinnia, Jim and Candy, a good Christian upbringing, and encouraged them to always do their best in school. With their encouragement, all four children completed high school and attended university. Marie and Tony provided the key that allowed their children to open the door to the storehouse of opportunity.

So many times, when I would go visit, I would quiz her about how she was feeling, how her health was. I knew she was in a lot of pain and discomfort because her health was failing. She would quickly change the subject to her family, this was her reason for being! Her house was adorned with numerous pictures of each and everyone of you. It was at this time that a warm genuine sincere smile would appear, combined with a sparkle and a twinkle in her eye. She was so proud of each and everyone of you.

Her son, Bob was talking about her the other night, how his Mom went far beyond the call of duty, our hurt, her hurt, our gains, her gains, our failures, her failures. We were truly her life. We have to thank her for always being there for us, for her being the glue, the mortar that held our family together through thick and thin.

I know during the course of my life I have met many people, some rich, some nice, some even famous, but none as gracious or ladylike as our Auntie Marie, because she possesses the greatest characteristic that God can bestow on a person, the ability to place the welfare of others first and foremost in their mind. Auntie Marie had the uncanny ability to make all those around her feel loved and special. She made you feel like you were capable of doing great things, feeling uplifted. Auntie Marie loved words, loved scrabble, crossword puzzles and it appears she had her very own inspirational mini Bible, it served as her guiding light and on the first page written in the universal language of love was the word caring which manifested itself in many ways as community mentor, writing letters, untangling government bureaucracy for pensioners, students and neighbours alike. Lending a sympathetic ear of confidence - never to tired to listen. A trustworthy source of advice and compassion-turning faith into action, ever present willingness to help others.

Marie was a born sales person and took great pleasure in selling things for others on the trading post. She became a regular personality on CFOK Radio. She sold everything from jars to cars, and never wanted to receive any commission. To many people she was known by different names, cabbage roll lady, the perogy lady, apple lady, egg lady and you know the 2nd page of her personal dictionary of life was the word sharing.

There were few things Marie enjoyed more than sharing bread with someone, and that came in many forms...preparing meals for her family, friends and neighbours or when she was catering. I recall after a function many people would drop by the kitchen and pay her a compliment, at this point I found her to be cute and with a smile and humble look in her eye in a self effacing way she would say thank you. We all know why her food was so good don't we, because she prepared the food with her beautiful hands of sincere self forgetting, she baked it in the gentle oven of love and she brought it to full temperature with a kind and loving heart. Can't you see her now... St. Peter, come over, I'll make something nice for you to eat. I can't help but feel the Kingdom of Heaven is just a little more nutritionally satisfied since the arrival of our Auntie Marie.

You know in her own right she was a teacher and a tiller of the soil. A teacher, because the most important lessons we learn in life are at our mothers knee. A tiller of the soil in a way because throughout her family's life she was planting the roses in the very fertile soil of her children's very being - to be passed on to further generations.

Firstly she seeded the rose of love and sharing and caring - Auntie fertilized them with kindness and gentleness then followed by watering with the ideals of decency and determination. But most important of all she planted, she gave the greatest rose, the greatest gift any parent can give to her children, the beautiful rose of faith and belief in God - for she knew that faith is like an iron peg in frozen ground - immovable, insurmountable even against the strongest onslaught, never to leave her even in the most trying of times. These flowers, like the springtime of life, are blooming now, these great ideals that she taught.

Yes, some of her children have grown into very proficient and responsible school teachers themselves. These roses she seeded continue to live on in the lives of friends and acquaintances. But the most important and most beautiful flowers are the fact that her children have accepted and readily display her characteristics of selfless love, sharing and caring! Auntie Marie lives on!

Yes, now this great lady's field is full, so full, as we view the springtime of her life, I know I speak for everyone when I say we loved you and we will miss you. Till we meet again, Auntie Marie.

RICHARD ERNEST SEQUIN

FEBRUARY 5, 1944 - NOVEMBER 23, 1991

WRITTEN AND DELIVERED BY ROBERT OWENS

Come unto me, all ye that labour and are heavy laden,
and I will give you rest
Take my yoke upon you, and learn of me;
for I am meek and lowly in heart;
and ye shall find rest unto your souls.
For my yoke is easy and my burden is light.

Family and friends of Richard, I stand before you this morning with a mind in confusion and a heart in pain. The anguish and unbelief has been experienced by all of us. The events preceding this day cloud our minds and numb our souls. These few minutes I share with you are difficult, very difficult; however I thank family members for allowing me this precious opportunity to share my feelings of love and admiration for Richard. One does not seek this assignment, however I am gratified to be able to express myself this day in a way that is meaningful and special.

Richard was many things to many people... an employer, a partner, a dear friend, a son, a brother, a husband, a father. In whatever capacity we knew him best, we knew him to be generous, fair, caring and compassionate.

What is the measure of a man? Philosophers and other learned men have pondered the contributions of many of those who have passed from mortality and extolled their wisdom, their abilities, and their accomplishments. These are worthy attributes, however, I respectfully submit that much more important yardsticks truly gauge our efforts in this life. I believe Richard sensed this also. His love of family and friends was demonstrated in many ways. Despite a heavy self-imposed workload, Richard was compelled to share his available free time with others. Seldom would Richard devote time for personal pursuits, but would rather organize and spend time together with family and friends. He delighted in giving aid to others; he was generous and

76

shared all he had; he valued friendships; he loved his family. Indeed, as successful as Richard was in temporal ways, these successes were eclipsed by simple gifts to us. His was a gift of service; a hand of friendship; a sympathetic ear... all acts of love.

To Mom and "Pop" Seguin, we can not comprehend the loss you feel this date. It is every parent's silent prayer that no child will depart this life before them. And yet some comfort must be found in knowing a child has returned to his Father in Heaven with honour and dignity. To have been entrusted to conceive, nurture and raise one of our Heavenly Father's children is a great blessing; to rear six children is a test and a challenge; to have raised this united, strong, caring family is testimony of your sacrifice and love.

Gail, we have been touched by your selfless dedication to your beloved husband over the recent weeks. It is apparent that the total focus of your being has been directed to Richard. No husband could have expected more; no wife could have provided more.

As Family and friends, we were awed by your courage; grateful for the exquisite care rendered to Richard. To me, the care administered by your hands was a manifestation of the loving care we all wished for Richard, but were each unable to provide in his time of need. Even in his eleventh hour I know in my heart Richard sensed your presence and was comforted.

The word "Father" has taken on an added dimension for three young people this day. No longer is father a source of encouragement, counsel and advice. For years Richard has been a conduit for guidance and knowledge. Each of you have been a receptacle for his insight and experience. The time has regrettably come when you must begin to take inventory of those treasures he has provided . Ponder and reflect upon his hopes and expectations for each of you. Recall and commit to memory those precious moments you have shared together. These memories will bring you joy. Remember as you grow older, you will understand and get to know your father even more than you do now.

For us, we must contemplate the future. A future that has been tarnished. Ever since Saturday in my mind I have heard Richard say "Look Bob, I had a good life...I had many reasons to live... it was not to be... but I had a good life." Richard does not lie in this casket... the spirit of Richard now dwells in peace and awaits the day when we can all be united. I believe that the Lord just acquired the best foreman and expeditor that he has ever had. I also believe that things are probably just a little better organized in the Kingdom of Heaven these past few days.

I believe we must all attempt to set aside for a minute our personal grief and consider how blessed we have been to have had the privilege of living in the presence of Richard. We have all benefited from the life of this man. He enriched our life. He lightened our load. He brightened our days. We knew Him. We loved him. Let us pray rather that all of us at some time enriched his life; lightened his load; brightened his day. I pray he knew us... and most importantly understood and knew of our love for him.

AMEN

VIRGINIA CURTIS

SEPTEMBER 30, 1947 - NOVEMBER 7, 1996

WRITTEN AND DELIVERED BY LEO SEGUIN

Family and Friends of Virginia. Virginia Curtis was many things to many people - a wife, a mother, a loving friend and confidante. In whatever capacity we knew her we know her to be gentle, warm, loving, caring, non-judgmental and humble. These common threads were woven from the strands of service to others before self.

Virginia Curtis was born in Medicine Hat on September 30, 1947 to Elvina and Albert Krauss, she has a brother Greg, and a sister Sylvia. While working at the Bank of Commerce she met her future life's partner, Bill. They were married on August 6, 1966. They were blessed with two boys, Billy Jr. and David. These two boys quickly became the heart and substance of their existence.

One thing I think we all know about Virginia was her remarkable God given artistic and creative talent. This professed itself in inspiring art work, beautiful signs and compelling and sincere teaching skills. In fact I think it would be safe to say she herself the person was a beautiful individual painted by the Master Artist himself, painted in the brightest of colours to reflect her cheerful, sunny enthusiastic disposition.

Family (embossed in gold) was the pride of that landscape and one of the most beautiful parts of her canvas. To be trusted by our God above with raising children is without doubt one of life's great adventures, and can quite often be the measure of one's own success. If this is true, Bill and Virginia through your dedication and determination you have truly achieved this high goal, for you have raised two fine, confident, mature, optimistic, loving individuals. Virginia was so proud of her two boys, Billy Jr. and David and now her daughter-in-law Kristen, she loved you all unconditionally and she praised you at every opportunity. She was so happy that David had found such a wonderful life's partner in Kristen. The night of the wedding Virginia was the happiest she had been for a long time!

Billy Jr. and David were in turn very proud of their Mother. They were talking the other night about their Mother always being patient and understanding, who would always take the time no matter how busy she was to give them a little advice, or a few words of wisdom, if we happened to fall behind in our studies, or if we strayed from the beaten path, her words were never stinging or violent, they couldn't very well be, for she was so gentle, so warm, yet her words carried more weight and were stronger than any giant's we've ever met. Bill Sr. said it best I think when he mentioned the boys could never of had a better Mother!

A major part of this divine portrait of Virginia was the word- friendship. Punctually, as many of you knew was not a strong suite for Virginia, but probably for good reason- no matter how busy she was she always made time for her friends. For many to have one true friend in life is a treasure, but the fact Virginia had so many genuine, sincere, loving friends is testament to a great person. Some of her friends comments about her - never thinks of herself, listens sincerely, sensitive, sincere, really cares, optimistic, positive, always places other's needs before her own, makes us feel special, never said an unkind word about anyone, would do anything for us.

The Good Lord must have had real trouble painting Virginia wouldn't you agree, because she never sat around long enough for that to happen, she was always on the move, raising money for M.S. through cycling 100 km, winning the top prize one year, a volunteer for Victim Services, visiting shut-ins (especially one lady on a regular basis). She loved to work for MOP, Moms of Pre-Schoolers, she loved to teach youngsters especially about art in this program. She was also involved in the Art Club, the Anglican Church and supported the boys as they went through golfing and swimming lessons, but possibly most important she was a great neighbour and second Mom to all the neighbour kids, a Block Parent before the word was even invented. When the Curtis Family opened a major Westlock recreation area in their back yard by investing in a trampoline, the Curtis home was a beehive of activity. Virginia gave freely of hugs, hospitality, food, cookies, first aid, kindness, respect and love. A selfless home where no one was turned away, the door was never locked and her heart was always open.

Virginia's career choice was a wise one, because her art work, the sign business were known throughout the community as first class, she had an eye for visualization, like I have never seen before. If you gave her a concept, an idea, she was so creative, so talented, she quickly turned it into something concrete, that was far beyond what you had ever expected. Many times I would go to her shop, perfectly satisfied with the work she had done, yet Virginia would not let it go, because it didn't meet her own high standards.

So what is this essence of life that sets this portrait, this masterpiece apart from so many others. Could it be the profound unique snow-white colour of faith. Faith for Virginia was selfless yet so powerful. It's ironic isn't it that November 11th today, Remembrance Day, is symbolic of courage, bravery, of unwavering steadfastness, like an oak tree, such was the nature of Virginia's faith as she confronted this most wicked of diseases. Always positive, never hateful, never complaining, never wanting to upset, never wanting to worry, never wanting to bother.

Virginia's talented brush of life touched so many of us. It lives on through her beautiful portraits, her beautiful signs, through her loving family, through her loyalty and devotion to her friends.

In closing maybe the best we could do is continue to paint some pictures in her honour, in her memory, open your home to a neighbourhood child, visit a shut-in (as Virginia did on a regular basis), extend a hand of friendship to someone new, to love your spouse more, we say goodbye to you now, Virginia, as you take your rightful place with the Master Artist himself in his Heavenly Art Gallery!

ORDER FORM

YES, PLEASE RUSH ME
_____ COPIES @ $ 9.95 = _____

POSTAGE AND HANDLING
_____ COPIES @ $ 3.00 = _____

SUB TOTAL   _____

G.S.T   _____

TOTAL   _____

METHOD OF PAYMENT:
(CHECK METHOD YOU WANT TO USE)

ENCLOSED IS MY CHEQUE/MONEY

PLEASE CHARGE MY CREDIT CARD ACCOUNT AS SHOWN

      VISA   MASTERCARD

CARD NUMBER: _____

EXPIRY DATE: _____

SHIP TO:

NAME: _____

ADDRESS: _____

_____

CITY: _____

PROV./STATE: _____

POSTAL/ZIP CODE: _____

TELEPHONE: AREA CODE: (_____) _____